The Lure of the Striped Pig

THE ILLUSTRATION OF
POPULAR MUSIC IN AMERICA
1820–1870

The Lure of the Striped Pig

THE ILLUSTRATION OF

POPULAR MUSIC IN AMERICA

1820-1870

by David Tatham

Imprint Society · Barre, Massachusetts · 1973

INTRODUCTION

I

The Art of Music Illustration

IT has always been the practice of man to ornament those things he has held to be of special worth, and music, both written and printed, has been no exception. Indeed, the limited number of note shapes and other music symbols which march along unbending staffs virtually cry out for visual relief. From ancient times until the rise of printed music in the sixteenth century, pictures were added to manuscripts by copyists for purely decorative reasons and also to illustrate some of the feelings and ideas the copyists and others had encountered in performances. When the printing of music became common, pictures continued to be added as decorations and illustrations. They conveyed something of the nature of the music to those who could not read the title or notation and intimated how the music might be performed to those who could read it. There were other reasons for the pictorial decoration of music, but by the early years of the nineteenth century, all had been subsumed in good part by the only reason which mattered any longer: pictures existed to enhance the sale of music to a wide public.

The American practice of music illustration began to flourish at this point. As the commercial enterprise of popular music publication grew vigorously, so also did the art of music illustration which served it. For about fifty years, from 1820 to 1870, American music illustrators imaginatively appealed to the lively taste of their countrymen for wonder, adventure, sentiment, and most of all, humor, expressed in pictures. The extensive body of prints which resulted contain hundreds of pictures which, while interesting in themselves as documents of the times, are of special significance as evidence of the response of one art to another, of pictorial artists to the world of music.

Pictorial representation is not the only means of music decoration, to be sure. From earliest to most recent times music has been ornamented with illuminated initial letters, calligraphic caption titles, and borders of printers' flowers, to mention a few examples. The present survey, however, focuses upon that sort of decoration which consists primarily of pictorial representation of one or another aspect of the music it accompanies. There was much of this in America during the years of our survey, and its ancestry, like that of the people who bought it, was European.

At the end of the fifteenth century, there were two main sorts of music illustration: the decoration of a page of the music, usually in the region of the caption title above the first stave, and the decoration of a title page for a book of music. Each form of pictorial decoration had its own conventions of style and imagery derived for use with printed music from the art of manuscript decoration. An artist who set out to pictorially decorate the score itself, at its heading or elsewhere, was reasonably expected to provide a picture which described something of the music it adorned. Most often he did this by placing a vignette—a small, borderless picture—with the caption title at the top of the first page of the music. His picture described the title, text, mood, or some other aspect of the music. The general term for this sort of illustration is *title vignette*. A good laconic American example is found on *Hunters of Kentucky* (pl. 3).

A different sort of illustration resulted when an artist set out to decorate a title page for a book consisting of several pieces of music, or one long piece of varied sections such as a mass. Since a full page was now involved, the design was larger and usually had well defined borders relating to the margin of the page. For subject matter, the artist could select one aspect from the music's variety or, as was more often done, he could provide a design which in its generality avoided specific reference to the music of the collection and portrayed instead such universally applicable images as gatherings of muses and assemblages of musical instruments. The term for this sort of design is *pictorial title page* and it is also known by the less explicit phrase *music title. The Dawning of Music in Kentucky* (pl. 1) is a particularly fine American example.

There was no reason, of course, that a collection of music could not have both a pictorial title page and caption title vignettes for the separate pieces, and many did. Both forms coexisted for generations and were joined early in the nineteenth century by a third form, which, though derived from the older types, served a special purpose for the newly burgeoning business of popular music publication. It was a pictorial title page, but not for a collection. Like the title vignette, its pictorial subject matter was specifically descriptive.

The roots of this new style of popular music decoration run back at least to George Bickham Jr.'s *Musical Entertainer*. This famous publication was a series of songs issued in London between 1736 and 1739 in fortnightly numbers consisting of four engraved folio sheets printed on one side only, usually one song to a sheet, each of which was charmingly decorated with an elaborate title vignette. In 1737 the first hundred plates (eighty-nine songs) were collected into a single volume with an added pictorial title page of the old style by Bickham Jr. and three pages of decorative calligraphy extolling the virtues of the art of music, engraved by George Bickham Sr. After the second hundred plates had been published, at the usual rate, they too were issued as a bound collection, in 1739. The songs were substantial and charming, with music adapted from Handel, Purcell, and Corelli among others and lyrics from Congreve, Gay, and less celebrated poets. Graced with Bickham's decorations, the *Entertainer* was ideally suited for display in a rococo music room where it would show at once the owner's refined taste in the musical and visual arts alike. The deserved popularity of the *Entertainer* was such that both volumes were reprinted in 1740 and again in 1765. Copies reached colonial America where they were treasured and set a standard for decorative engraving never approached by native artisans during the rest of the century. In England, where Bickham was but one of a number of capable artist-engravers always overshadowed by Hogarth, the *Entertainer* was universally acknowledged as the best of its kind.

The special importance of the *Entertainer* to our present interests rests with Bickham's invariable rule that descriptive pictorial matter must appear on every page to illustrate some aspect of the music of the page. When a song required more than one page, as with *A Cypress Grove [Myrtillo]* which runs to four, Bickham provided the usual title vignette for the first page and then a different illustration for each of the succeeding pages. Though Bickham's rule was hardly ever again practiced so rigorously, his work nevertheless exerted a strong influence on the development of popular music illustration. He had demonstrated that popular song, carefully illustrated in high fashion, sold well to the general public. He had also established that descriptive illustrations were more appealing than abstract decoration and indeed that some of the public bought the *Entertainer* for its pictures rather than for its music. With Bickham, whose chief motive had always been to tap middle-class pocketbooks, we find the origins of modern ideas about how printed popular music should be decorated.

The songs of the *Entertainer* were brief and simply set, consisting most often of a vocal line with figured bass for harpsichord and usually a flute part placed by itself at the bottom of the single page. By the early years of the nineteenth century this format was inadequate for most popular music for a number of reasons, not the least of which was the practice of publishing songs with fully harmonized piano parts. With a single page now insufficient, and the printing of both sides of the sheet impractical because it required the performer to turn mid-way through the piece, a new format was needed. During the decades flanking the turn of the nineteenth century, a variety of formats saw use. Common in America was a folded sheet providing four quarto pages with the music printed on pages 2 and 3, making the whole score visible when laid flat. The caption title and vignette (if any) were on page 2. The outer surfaces of the sheet, pages 1 and 4, remained blank, thus requiring the opening of the folder to see what the music might be, an awkward arrangement for the person hunting through a stack for a particular piece. Later the title and its vignette began to appear on page 1 while the music began on page 2 or 3, running to what additional leaves were necessary. Among other things, this development reflected the willingness of publishers and buyers to invest more of their resources to achieve higher standards of design in printed music—to reach toward Bickham's decorative standard though not toward the actual appearance and compact format of the *Entertainer* plates. Though caption title vignettes continued in use, title pages were seen more often during the first decades of the century. Most consisted of a decorated title, the publisher's imprint, and a vignette descriptive of the music. The vignette was typically in the manner of the caption title vignette, though larger. This was a true and proper title page, though for a single piece of popular music rather than for a collection.

In the ensuing years the vignette became an ever larger component of the title page until it ceased to be a true vignette. Elaborate surrounds, subsidiary vignettes, and picture frame borders all served to

extend the pictorial matter. In time most of the area of the page came to be taken up by a single large picture. Finally, the entire page was captured by the picture which now incorporated the title, imprint, and other lettered matter into the pictorial design. This progress from caption title vignette, to title page vignette, to large illustration, and at last to full page is seen in plates 3, 10, 44, and 56. The colorful full page "covers" of the 1850s and later, such as plate 34, are indeed pictorial title pages, though of the newer kind. Their ancestry derives, as we have said, mainly from the vignette rather than from the more generalized pictorial title page for collections of music.* Of course, the development was not as simple as our summary may suggest. The small vignette never disappeared entirely and fascinating hybrids of vignette and full page pictures abound. What is clear is that between 1820 and 1870, the pictorial matter of popular music assumed ever greater importance to publishers who accordingly gave over an ever greater portion of the title page to it. This was by no means a distinctively American phenomenon; at every point in the development of music illustration American publishers and artists followed the example of British music, which, it might be added, had been influenced by French solutions to the challenges of design. Though this resulted in a basic international style of decoration, each nation's artists found ways to give a special native flavor to their finished products.

The rapid development from caption vignette to poster-like title page in America was made possible

* Since the middle of the last century, pictorial title pages for music have popularly been called *covers*, doubtless because they are in some ways analogous to book and magazine covers. Even though the meaning of the term is clear enough and its brevity has earned it near-universal usage, there remains an important distinction to be made between a cover and a title page, and for two reasons. First, publishers ordinarily thought of the pictorial title page as page 1 and numbered succeeding pages accordingly. Second, from the 1840s through the Civil War much popular music was issued with colored paper wrappers, which are covers of a sort, the purpose of which was to keep music clean at sellers' shops and to broadcast the title, which was frequently printed in large letters on the front wrapper. It is unusual to find them intact today; owners seem to have stripped them off soon after buying the music. In rare instances, pictorial matter was printed on the wrappers and it is in such cases that a distinction needs to be maintained between the wrappers and the title page.

by the phenomenal growth of the business of music publishing. The publishing boom resulted from the rapidly expanding population, of course, but also from the fervor with which middle class families embraced the beliefs and accouterments of genteel taste. As soon as a stretch of wilderness was cleared, pianos were carted through to the more prosperous homes, where they offered an element of yearned-for culture and a stay against the rudeness of the frontier. In both the settlements of the West and the cities of the East, a talent for music became the *sine qua non* for proper young ladies. Whether nature had furnished the requisite musical gifts was not a serious consideration. What mattered was that the canons of genteel child-rearing be followed. Fresh music on the piano and hours of practice signified that knowing parents were guiding their young upward along the path to an American Parnassus.

Part of that journey would have been danced after 1830, for with the appearance of the polka in that decade, soon followed by the waltz, mazurka, schottische, galop, and others, America became enamored of the couple dance. Dance music became the worthy companion to song in the repertoire of polite young ladies, and thereby created a lucrative new line for publishers, who exploited the possibilities by bringing out dance numbers for piano named after towns, schools, popular idols, and novelties of any sort that might appeal to ladies' fancies. Beyond the general effect of a national determination to acquire cultivated manners, other forces contributed to a growing demand for published music. For example, the efforts of most American religious groups, beginning in the eighteenth century, to foster universal musical literacy resulted early in the nineteenth century in a vast population to whom printed music was part of everyday life. From these and other influences grew a demand for new music so great that by the 1840s the business of music publication, which earlier had been a high-risk profession, became a means of amassing a substantial fortune.

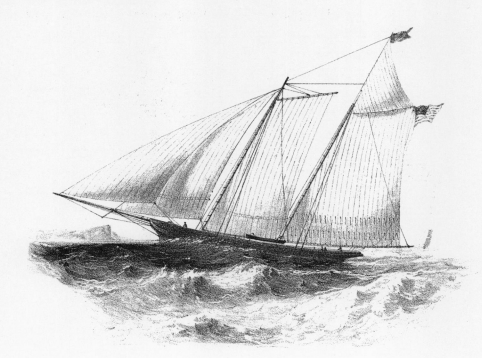

Music publication would doubtless have flourished without pictorial decoration, but that so much music came to be illustrated in these years resulted from the arrival of lithographic printing in America. The use of the process for illustration was actually the outgrowth of a search for a new method of printing the music itself. Printing by movable type was the oldest method, dating from the fifteenth century, but problems of setting music type were difficult enough so that except for such simple music as served hymnals, the method was not commonly used after engraving was established in the seventeenth century as the standard means of printing music. Engraving produced eminently satisfactory music (it still does) but it was sufficiently expensive and time consuming so that printers and publishers kept looking for methods which were cheaper and faster. When such a method arrived at the very end of the eighteenth century in the form of lithography, it was thought that it would soon supplant engraving. In theory it was the ideal method. A score could be written out with special ink on special paper, then transferred to the printing stone and fixed chemically, and thousands of impressions could be had. In practice, however, the lithographed scores, even when prepared by the best copyists, lacked the sharpness and clarity of engraving and so lithography was only occasionally used after its early trials. A comparison of the lithographed *Maid of the Rock* (pl. 2) with the engraved page from *Hunters of Kentucky* (pl. 3) shows the difference.

To the pictorial artist, on the other hand, lithography presented exciting new possibilities. He could now execute his own design and have it reproduced as he had drawn it, without the intercession of an engraver to translate the drawing to a series of lines and dots. The freshness and immediacy of an original drawing, and the full range of its tonal gradations, reproduced easily. Because lithography was cheaper than engraving for most applications, and had advantages for the illustrator, American title pages were printed by lithography more often than not after 1826. If a piece with a lithographed title page were also to have a caption vignette on the first page of music, it would be engraved along with the music. If in addition the piece were to have wrappers, they would be printed by letterpress and the publication would then encompass all three of the major commercial printing processes of the day.

The relative cheapness of lithographed illustrations encouraged a broadening of the uses of printed music. It now came to be issued as political campaign pieces, souvenirs of resorts, memorials to loved ones, and commemorative devices for social clubs, to mention but a few examples. Embellished with suitable pictures, these pieces were published for reasons having little to do with musical merit and were prized by persons who never performed them. Plates 21, 44, and 58 are examples.

As the major publishers prospered, their need for new music quickened. Their best sellers turned stale about as quickly as do hit phonograph recordings in the twentieth century. Although publishers maintained stables of native tunesmiths and versemakers, the best pool of talent was in England. In the absence of international copyright conventions—there were none until 1891 between England and the United States—any British publication was available to any American publisher for the taking. Major American publishers had agents in London who, as soon as a piece of music began to capture English fancy, dispatched a copy by fast ship to America. When a publisher chose to gamble on an American edition, he usually arranged to have the pictorial matter copied along with the music. German and French music was pirated as well, though often by way of English editions with English illustrations.

Raiding of this sort was not an exclusively American activity by any means. Minstrel songs of the 1840s were snapped up by British publishers who sometimes fitted them out with new illustrations by the talented array of artists available to them. As the songs of Henry Russell, the most popular composer and singer in America in the early 1840s, went through multiple editions here, publishers in his native Britain brought them out as well. In his case the American illustrations were more often adapted, perhaps because he had been so well served by Fitz Hugh Lane and Benjamin Champney. Nor was the pirating of illustrations solely a trans-Atlantic affair; Americans copied Americans, usually when the publication was not copyrighted but sometimes when it was. From these examples we get some idea of the extent to which publishers felt that the success of an unauthorized

"But here was old Kentucky."

"A Gentlemen & Ladies fair"

an artist's drawing, could be reproduced endlessly. But the development was extremely slow. Not until the late 1850s were satisfactory results obtained with any regularity by the early American practitioners. It seems likely that the pictorial title for the *Wheelbarrow Polka* (pl. 43) was to be illustrated with a photolithograph but that something went amiss, leaving the job to Winslow Homer. Things continued to go amiss so far as the development of photolithography was concerned, with the result that it did not come into general use for music decoration until well after the close of our period.

In general, the music illustrators of the second generation were better trained from the outset than had been their predecessors. The rising standard of draughtsmanship was largely responsible, no doubt, for the withdrawal of the prolific John H. Bufford as an active illustrator after the early 1850s. The ever-increasing demands of managing a large printing shop had much to do with it but so also must have an awareness that his own limited skills were no match for the virtuoso draughtsmen of the new generation. Bufford sought young lads with budding talents in drawing and took them on as apprentices, much as he himself had begun at the Pendleton shop in 1829. Between 1855 and 1857, three of his apprentices were Winslow Homer, Joseph Foxcroft Cole, and Joseph E. Baker. Homer left the Bufford shop as soon as his twenty-first birthday arrived and within a year had gained a national following as an illustrator for the pictorial press, while edging slowly toward the career in painting which in time made him perhaps the best known and most widely admired of American artists. Cole too left as soon as his apprenticeship ended and embarked on a successful career as a landscape painter. Only Baker remained with the Bufford firm, becoming its chief music illustrator and continuing in that role well into the 1870s. At the outset he seems to have been very much under the pictorial influence of his good friend Homer, treating in a similar fashion subjects which Homer favored in his work, such as the vogue for ice-skating (pl. 46). Like Homer, Baker's early style often had an element of caricature to it, as we see in *I Would I Were A Slave Again* (pl. 52). Later in the 1860s, many of Baker's drawings are awash with maudlin sentiment, the mood of the subject matched by a free, soft focus manner of drawing which contrasts with his earlier work and his non-sentimental designs such as the *Velocipede Galop* of 1869. Baker's sentimentalism has long been out of favor and seems painfully excessive to modern eyes. Yet he was almost

always original, and at his best his work is only a cut below Homer's. Only a small portion of Baker's work can be considered his best, however, and his worst work is abundant.

Homer himself worked at music illustration for about two years. When taken on at age eighteen by Bufford, Homer's very first assignment was to copy illustrations for new editions of old songs. There seems to be nothing of Homer in these. He then drew illustrations for at least nine other title pages, most of which are adapations from existing designs, but containing important original elements, as we see in *The Ratcatcher's Daughter* (pl. 41). A number of other Bufford music titles of 1855–1857 may also be Homer's work, at least in part, but are unsigned.

A good many other artists of considerable ability were active in the 1850s. It would be good to know more of Emile Masson (pls. 39 and 53) who had a flair for the comic. M. Schmitz of Philadelphia was a splendid copyist and some of his designs may be original. James Queen is a puzzle, for though he was a capable original artist (pl. 35), like Schmitz he seems to have been employed chiefly as a copyist. It is maddening to see how abjectly he copied faults as well as strengths. What imagination Queen seems to have lacked was possessed in ample supply by one of his competitors in Philadelphia in the 1850s, John L. Magee, who inexplicably seems never to have applied his inventive mind to music illustration. What few title pages are known to be his work are copies from British music or lacklustre portraits, done we suspect to turn a dollar. There is just a bit of his comic style in the grotesque elements of the *Ledger Polka* (pl. 48), but not enough to justify confident attribution to him.

Of the many varied subjects of the 1850s, perhaps no single topic was treated so often as the singer Jenny Lind during her Barnum-promoted tours. European royalty was another favorite topic, at least until 1861, when the Civil War cooled the North's relations with England enough to dissuade publishers from gambling on pieces which sported idealized portraits of Victoria or the Prince of Wales. The Civil War itself, of course, was the great subject of the 1860s. The hundreds of pieces of popular music generated by the long conflict include many comic and sentimental songs which differ from non-war songs only in their topicality. Most of them apply equally well to the North and the South, despite their surface partisanship. The deeply partisan patriotic pieces are different, however, particularly in their postures of unalloyed righteousness. They express the sort of unthinking patriotism

that properly worried Lincoln and others who anticipated that the binding up of the nation's wounds
would be a greater task than the winning of the war.
Because most of the presses and the rest of the ma-
chinery of music publication were concentrated in the
North, the great majority of war pieces boom the
Union cause, though they do not exceed the Confed-
erate pieces in the stridency of their partisanship. The
songs of the victorious North became, even before the
close of the war, foundation deposits in what Robert
Penn Warren has called the "Treasury of Virtue" from
which the nation has ever since drawn moralistic
jingos for its war efforts. The glorification of war which
is found in many of the illustrations contrasts ironi-
cally with the unglamorous scenes of army camp life
shown in the pictorial press. The contrast is greater
still with the chilling photographs of battlefield car-
nage by Mathew Brady and others.

After the war, an exhausted nation refreshed itself
with games of croquet, fancy dress balls, and vogues
for velocipedes, all dutifully depicted by music illustrators (pls. 56 and 58). These illustrations are less
dependent on British style due not only to the waning
of English influences during the war, but also to the
maturing of the American arts, illustration included.
This is one reason why the great British music illustrator Alfred Concanen, who was at the height of his fame
during the post-war years, was so little copied. The
other reason, we might note, is that Concanen specialized more than any of his contemporaries in a very
narrow range of London subjects, subjects which did
not travel well.

In the decade after 1870, the popular music industry
continued to thrive, issuing ever-larger editions of
popular music, but the art of illustrating that music
went into decline. The qualities which had been most
appealing to previous generations, and which are most
appealing to twentieth century eyes, gradually disappeared. Primitivism in native art seemed to embar-
rass rather than charm. Gone was the evidence of an
artist struggling with his medium and gone as well was
direct printing from the surface on which the artist
had drawn—that quality which made each title page
an original print. All of this was replaced by often

ill-designed and poorly printed photographic repro-
ductions of art work which was itself commonly tired
and inappropriate. This is not to say that American
music illustration after 1880 is a wasteland, for there
are a few graceful and inventive designs to be found in
any year, and especially in the decades flanking the
turn of the century. But the tastes and technologies of
the art of music illustration are so vastly changed after
1880 from what they were before 1870, that it is clear
that a new era has opened and that comparisons between the new and the old will be difficult to make.

Between 1910 and 1950, there arose a large and
important body of popular song in the innovative
works of Jerome Kern, Irving Berlin, George and Ira
Gershwin, Cole Porter, Richard Rodgers and Lorenz
Hart, and a handful of others. But even the great merit
of this music was not enough to revive the art of music
illustration. The best efforts were made in the 1930s
by *New Yorker* artists and others working in a linear
graphic style, but these amount to theatre posters
which advertise musical comedies more than they
illustrate songs. Attempts to deal with individual
songs were uncommon—Constantin Alajalov's work
for *George Gershwin's Song Book* (1932) and John
Held Jr.'s illustrations for *Frankie and Johnny* (1930)
and other old ballads soar above most other efforts.
America's golden age of popular song was served in
the main by unimaginative, ill-conceived designs.
Indeed, during these same years the public's very
need for printed music slowly diminished with the
encroachments of radio and the phonograph and the
rise of largely improvised music such as jazz. The now
moribund art of title page design limped on as editions
grew smaller, showing barely a glimmer of the freshness and imagination which had enlivened the sheet
music of the previous century. By 1960 it was clear
that the best possibilities for music illustration were
not offered by printed music at all but rather by the
new art of long-playing record jacket design, an art
more closely allied to poster design than to the older
traditions of music decoration. Those older traditions
had been so firmly rooted in their times that there was
no way to transplant them. Having served their pur-
poses, they had passed into history.

PLATES

WHEN a freshly printed supply of new music arrived at the store of its publisher, each copy was virtually identical to every other copy in the issue. As soon as the publisher commenced distribution of the copies, they began to acquire the marks and signs of wear which in time constituted the evidence of a long and interesting history. The publisher first placed some copies on sale at his own shop, usually not marking them since his imprint and price were printed on each copy. If the work were to be copyrighted, he deposited two copies at the clerk's office of the District Court which served his area, and the clerk duly inscribed the date of the deposit on each copy. The publisher then delivered quantities of the piece to other music sellers in his city and shipped batches to sellers in other cities as well, where the name of the local shop was often stamped on the face of each copy. These dealers in turn supplied the notion shops and general stores which served as purveyors of music for the hinterlands. The publisher meanwhile delivered complimentary copies to local newspapers and periodicals, expecting to have notice taken of them in listings of new publications. He advertised his new music—especially those with pictorial title pages—in his shop window, as we see in plate 35, and did whatever he could to have his most likely hits plugged by performance at concerts in theatres, on town commons, in dancing classes, and wherever popular music might be played. He seems also to have anticipated the book trade by scheduling composers' autograph parties.

Many of the pieces reproduced in the following pages show specific evidence of what happened to them after leaving the publisher's shop. Such marks as a music seller's stamp, a composer's autograph, the owner's name, a library accession mark, a copyright deposit inscription, and marginalia of various sorts supply clues to the history of an individual piece and are invaluable to the sleuthing scholar. Several of the title pages have a torn left margin, showing that the piece has been disbound. In such cases we may be confident that the other three margins were trimmed at the time of binding, perhaps by as much as half an inch on each side from the original dimensions of the printed sheet. Those dimensions were, for most of the years covered here, about ten and a half by fourteen and a quarter inches (26.8 x 36.3 cm.). Though this torn and trimmed condition is lamentable, its cause— the practice of binding personal collections of sheet music—is responsible for the preservation of a great deal of the music of the era. During these years, ladies from time to time assembled a number of favorite pieces and had them bound to keep them in order and out of harm's way. The bindings were fine things, typically consisting of gold tooled leather spines, decorated boards, and marbled end-papers, with the owner's name stamped in gold on a label on the front cover. If it had not been bound, much of the music of the era would have been discarded along with old magazines as both became dated, but if the music seemed dispensable, the bindings were for the ages, or so it seemed, and the volumes were preserved, if seldom opened. In the twentieth century when the music and its illustrations took on new value as important relics of cultural history, many collections were disbound so that the individual pieces might be sold to collectors. With ragged left margins, these pieces resumed their independent lives after more than a century.

I have dated the illustrations on the basis of the following information: copyright notices printed on the music; copyright entry books and deposit copies at the Library of Congress; addresses of publishers and printers; publishers' plate number series; biographical information concerning the artists; dates as part of artists' signatures; and internal information from the illustration itself. None of these sources is absolutely faultless. For example, illustrations were prepared for new editions of music that had been copyrighted in an earlier year. Further, some artists' illustrations saw service on more than one publication, often years apart. At worst, the dates I have assigned should not be off by more than a year and in most cases I believe them to be quite accurate.

Because this is a listing of prints rather than music, the title given at each entry is that shown on the print. It is the title which the artist would most likely have known. To aid in locating copies of the music, basic facts of publication, and a caption title when it differs from what is on the title page, are given for each entry. Dimensions for the illustrations, height before width, are given in centimeters for the image, not including ruled borders or detached decorative surrounds. The location of the copy reproduced is given at the close of each entry. It should be remembered that variant states of some of the illustrations exist and that other editions of some of the music were issued with different title pages, sometimes without illustrations. Moreover, some of the illustrations reproduced here were later used with other music and in those cases the illustrations often were thoroughly re-drawn. Wolfe numbers refer to Richard J. Wolfe's bibliography *Secular Music in America 1801–1825* (New York: New York Public Library, 1964).

MASSA GEORGEE WASHINGTON

AND

General La Fayette.

As Sung, in Character, by Mr ROBERTS, with unrivalled applause;

at the

THEATRE, CHATHAM GARDENS.

Written & Composed by,

Micah Hawkins.

NEW YORK;

Engraved, Printed, & Sold, by, E. Riley, 29, Chatham Street

5 David Claypoole Johnston (1798–1865),
The Log House, 1826.

Lithograph, printed by William and John Pendleton, Boston, 14 x 21.4.
Music by Anthony Philip Heinrich; words by John Mills Brown. Boston: the
    composer, 1826.
American Antiquarian Society.

The modest fame garnered for Heinrich by the publication of his
Dawning (pl. 1) assured a warm welcome when he moved from Kentucky to Boston in 1823. He soon became a central figure in the small
but congenial concert life of the city, and for three years he taught,
composed, and concertized. In September 1826 he sailed for Europe,
hoping to be reunited with his daughter and to try his skills in the far
more demanding musical competition there. At a farewell concert in
Boston, he performed *The Log House,* his own setting of verses (by
J. M. Brown) about his year at Bardstown, Kentucky. Heinrich
published the song with an elaborate title page—the first, it might be
noted, to be printed by lithography in America.

Heinrich and D. C. Johnston were probably acquainted as early as
February 1821, when the composer took leave of Kentucky for a few
weeks to supply music for the melodrama *Child of the Mountain* at
Philadelphia's Walnut Street Theatre. Johnston's father was in charge
of the box office and the artist himself, already a professional engraver,
was rehearsing for his debut in another play on the same stage. For
The Log House, Johnston designed a title page which amounts to a
testimonial to the composer and to the musical results of his self-
imposed year of near-solitude in a Kentucky cabin. It seems quite clear
that Heinrich had a hand in determining what went into it; the lyrics
offer very little for an illustrator to work with. Amidst the assortment
of pictorial references mentioned earlier in this book, we see Heinrich's
log cabin near Bardstown on the occasion when his playing late at
night attracted a Negro stranger, who, having enjoyed the tune, offered
Heinrich a coin to play it again.

This title page exists in two states, of which ours is the earlier. In the
second state, a vignette has been added under the line "There first
lov'd Minstrelsy I woo'd" showing Heinrich at Boston harbor declaim-
ing "For England" as his coat tails are tugged in opposite directions
by a British lion and an American eagle.

THE LOG HOUSE

A Song, presented to the

Western Minstrel.

by John Mills Brown.

"The fields his Study —— Nature was his Book"
Bloomfield.

D.C.Johnston del.   Copyright secured.   Lith of Pendleton.

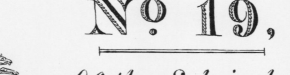

№ 19,

Of the Sylviad.

A. P. Heinrich

TO HIS LOG HOUSE.

"There first lov'd Minstrelsy I woo'd"

Boston March 14.th 1826

Throop Scrip.

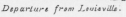

Departure from Louisville.   Arrival in Boston.

6 Unknown artist,
The Archer's March, 1829.

Lithograph, printed by Kennedy and Lucas, Philadelphia, 15.8 x 18.2.
Music by William H. W. Darley. Philadelphia: R. H. Hobson, 1829.
Collection of the author.

This archer, attired in the high fashion of his sport, glorifies the membership and ideals of the United Bowmen. Founded at Philadelphia in 1828 by a group including the artists Thomas Sully and Titian Ramsay Peale, the Bowmen began the practice of field archery as an organized amateur sport in America. The official costume for competitions at first included Lincoln Green frock coats and broad-brimmed straw hats topped with ostrich plumes. The garb shown here is far simpler and more practical. One of the members of the Bowmen may have designed this vignette, though other possibilities include Jane Cooper (Sully) Darley, daughter of the painter Thomas Sully and wife of the composer of *The Archer's March,* who was a prominent Philadelphia musician and the older brother of Felix O. C. Darley. Felix, who was to become one of the nation's foremost illustrators, is an unlikely candidate for the authorship of this design since he was only eight years old in 1829.

This piece is an early example of music published to commemorate an organization. In succeeding years the memberships and noble goals of volunteer firemen, rowing clubs, Masons, Odd Fellows, and the numerous private militia companies of the day were celebrated by the publication of marches, polkas, and quick steps, usually sporting title pages showing one or more idealized worthies of the organization.

The lettered title shown here is rather more simple than those which later emblazoned title pages of this sort. It is interesting to note that the symmetry of the title is broken slightly to avoid the collision of letters with the upraised bow, showing that the lettering was done after the vignette had been drawn on stone, which was the usual practice. Lettering on the title page—always drawn in reverse on the stone—was the work of a specialist at the larger lithographic printing shops.

THE ARCHERS MARCH

Composed, Arranged
for the
PIANO FORTE,

Kennedy & Lucas Lith.

And Respectfully Inscribed to the
UNITED BOWMEN
by
W. H. W. DARLEY
Member of the Association.

Philad.ᵃ Published by R.H.Hobson, 147 Chesnut St.
Entered according to act of Congress, July 8ᵗʰ 1829.

MAJOR JACK DOWNING'S MARCH

H. Inman. Del.

Composed & arranged

FOR THE

Piano Forte

Dedicated to the Second Brigade Downingville Militia

BY

J.T. NORTON.

May be had at all the music stores in the U. States.

Childs & Lehman Lith. Philadelphia.

11 Alfred Jacob Miller (1810–1874),
Far O'er the Deep Blue Sea, 1834.

Lithograph, printed by George Willig, 13.5 x 20.5.
Music by John H. Hewitt; words by R. H. Pratt. Baltimore: Geo. Willig, 1834.
American Antiquarian Society.

Between 1831 and 1834, Miller studied painting with Thomas Sully in Philadelphia and then at the École des Beaux-Arts in Paris and the American School at Rome. When he returned to his native Baltimore late in 1834, he set up painting rooms directly above the shop of George Willig, music printer and publisher. While struggling to become established as a painter of portraits, he designed at least two music titles for his landlord, perhaps, it has been suggested, to pay his rent. His signature is more explicit than was commonly the case with lithographic artists and so we know that the design is original and that the work on stone is by Miller as well. The vignette has a flavor of French illustration and may reflect some attention to the art during his sojourn in Paris.

Though the subject matter is not remarkable, Miller's handling of it is. Unlike the typical music illustrator of his day, he seems to have had real anatomy and real emotion in mind as he devised his design. This should be so, of course, since he was a well-trained professional artist of uncommon skill. In 1837 he traveled to the Rocky Mountains and made the studies of Indian life for which he is best known.

FAR O'ER THE DEEP BLUE SEA

Written by

R. H. PRATT ESQ,

Composed by

John H. Hewitt.

Price 50 Cents.

Baltimore Published by G. Willig Jr.

12   John H. Bufford (1810–1870),
Rangers' Trip to Westborough, 1834.

Lithograph, printed by William Pendleton, Boston, 13.4 x 22.2.
Music by James Hootin. Boston: C. Bradlee, 1834.
Harvard College Library.

During the 1830s, young men formed private, chartered militia companies in reaction to the unmilitary, slipshod operation of a state militia dominated by older officers whose memories of the War of 1812 held little interest for the younger generation. The private, or volunteer, companies required elegant uniforms of their members—at each man's expense—and prided themselves on the disciplined smartness of their parades, the colorfulness of their ceremonies, and the brilliance of the music commissioned for their bands. Much of this music came to be published for piano, usually with handsomely decorated title pages. The initial printing was doubtless paid for by subscription from members, though certain of the pieces became popular enough with the public to require several reprintings.

The lion, symbol of Boston's Rifle Rangers, watches as the company assembles for its first train ride. John Bufford, who was in his fifth year at the Pendleton shop, knew that Boston's premier hotel, the Tremont House, had no railroad running behind it, but since the illustration is allegorical and idealized, this sort of rearrangement of nature was allowable and made sense.

W. Rimmer, del.

THE FIREMAN'S CALL,

As Sung by

GEORGE WASHINGTON DIXON,

Respectfully Dedicated to the Officers and Members of the

Fire Department of Boston,

Music from the Opera of the Maid of Judah.

Boston: Published by C.H. Keith, 67 Court Street.

Entered according to Act of Congress in the Year 1827 by C.H. Keith, in the Clerks Office of ...

17 Fitz Hugh Lane (1804–1865),
    Captn. E. G. Austin's Quick Step, 1837.

Lithograph, printed by Thomas Moore, Boston, 15.6 x 24.6.
Music arranged by Thomas Comer. Boston: Parker & Ditson, 1837.
American Antiquarian Society.

As a cripple, Lane could be only an onlooker at the drills of this fashionably uniformed private militia company, and it is perhaps for this reason that so much of his effort was devoted to the background with its views of the U.S.S. *Constitution* and Boston beyond, the dome of Bulfinch's State House rising on the horizon. Though Lane has made all the volunteers look alike, we learn a good deal about how they considered themselves, for pieces such as this were essentially self-advertisements. The illustration is a key source of information about the size and composition of the volunteer company bands and is, in fact, among the earliest American prints showing a band of instrumentalists in performance.

This title page served two separate publications, *Captn. E. G. Austin's Quick Step* and *A Yankee Ship and a Yankee Crew.* Common title pages for two or more separately published compositions were often used in the 1840s and later, typically in the format shown in plates 30 and 42. Lane's design was appropriated by other publishers, notably by Firth & Hall in New York for the title page of Allen Dodworth's *Ocean Wave Quick Step* in 1843. The adapting artist, Charles Parsons (pl. 31) of the Endicott shop, altered the uniforms and changed the band's instrumentation, kept the *Constitution,* and transformed the skyline from Boston's to New York's.

CAPT.ᴺ E. G. AUSTIN'S QUICK STEP.

As first performed by the

BOSTON BRIGADE BAND ON THE ANNIVERSARY OF THE

BOSTON LIGHT INFANTRY,

MAY 31ˢᵀ 1837.

Also the New Nautical Song

A YANKEE SHIP AND A YANKEE CREW,

Sung by

MR. WILLIAMSON.

Words by J. S. JONES Esq. — Melody by C. M. KING Esq.

The whole arranged for the PIANO FORTE and dedicated to the

OFFICERS & MEMBERS OF THE B.L.I.

BY T. COMER.

Price 50 cts.

BOSTON Pubᵈ by PARKER & DITSON, 107 Washⁿ St.

Entered according to Act of Congress by PARKER & DITSON in the year 1837 in the Clerks office of the District Court of Mass.

18 George Sanford (act. c. 1837–c. 1847),
The Striped Pig, 1838.

Lithograph, printed by George Endicott, New York, 26.7 x 23.2.
Composer unknown. New York: Hewitt & Jaques.
American Antiquarian Society.

Compared with the dandified private companies, the state militia units of the 1830s presented a sorry spectacle of poorly drilled troops in makeshift uniforms whose buffoonery made a travesty of their supposed responsibilities as a home guard. When the local units assembled at the annual state musters, their faults multiplied, and worse still, what little military bearing was brought to the encampment soon washed away with the flow of whiskey and rum. Drunkenness became so common at the annual assemblies that the more practical of the temperance societies were believed to have exempted muster days from the otherwise comprehensive clauses of their abstinence pledges. The tone of the muster was expected to improve in 1838 in Massachusetts, since temperance interests there had succeeded in gaining the passage of a state law which prohibited the sale and purchase of spirits in any quantity less than fifteen gallons. Although the law was not aimed specifically at musters, it dulled the enthusiasm of most militiamen for that year's retreat since it effectively made the sale of liquor by the drink unlawful. But when the muster commenced at Dedham, it was soon clear that the law had been circumvented. Near the muster field, a local citizen had set up a tent to exhibit a rare striped pig—the stripes were alternating bands of red and black paint. For the price of admission to the exhibit, each viewer received a glimpse of a temporary marvel of nature, and a drink.

In reporting this comic incident, George Sanford focuses on the bedraggled militiamen and their improvised uniforms as much as on the drawing power of the most alluring pig of the age. The minor defects of the illustration, such as the poorly conceived background figures and a distracting expanse of foreground, are probably a result of Sanford's youthful inexperience, since his illustrations of the next few years show greater skill and subtlety—though to be sure, subtlety would have been lost on this subject. While Endicott artists of the 1830s and 1840s often dated their music illustrations, as we see in this case, the practice was highly unusual at other shops, where greater deference was paid to the publisher's maxim that music, like women, should not be dated. For this reason, copyright lines were lettered so small as to be practically unreadable.

DE OLE JAW BONE.

AS SUNG BY

MR J. W. SWEENY,

THE CELEBRATED BANJO PLAYER.

BOSTON.

Published by HENRY PRENTISS, 33 Court St.

Entered according to Act of Congress in the year 1840 by H. Prentiss in the Clerks office of the District Court of Massachusetts.

24 Benjamin Champney (1817–1907),
O Swift We Go, 1840.

Lithograph, printed with tint by Benjamin W. Thayer, Boston, 9.8 x 14.
Music by Joseph Philip Knight; words by J. T. Fields. Boston: Oakes & Swan, 1840.
Collection of the author.

After serving as an apprentice from 1834 to 1838, Champney worked as
a lithographic artist in Boston until 1841, when he left for France and
later success as a painter of a vast moving panorama of the Rhine
valley, and then long maturity as the dean of White Mountain land-
scapists. Of the small corpus of his work as a music illustrator, his best
achievements are to be found in the form of the small, intimate vignette, as we see here. Within this style he did not need to contend with
drawing the human figure in detail. Further, his sense of design had
room to place his illustration to best advantage on the page within
ample borders and to make good use of geometric tint patterns.
Patterns such as these were used chiefly in the first few years of tint-
printing—from about 1840 to 1843—and then they gave way to a style
in which the tint was drawn to form an integral part of the design.
Here, Champney has used it as a muted contrasting element.

The illustration is one of mood. The chill of winter is echoed in the
picturesquely twisted tree and softened by the warm greetings which
are waved between the boys and the sleigh passengers. The mammoth
sleigh is one of the fleet for which Boston was well-known in the middle
third of the century.

Later editions of this song were issued by Wm. Oakes and, in 1842, by
George P. Reed, both using Champney's title page. Some, if not all, of
the Reed title pages were printed without tint.

O SWIFT WE GO,

A SLEIGHING SONG.

R. Champney del.

the POETRY by

J. T. FIELDS Esq.

the Music composed and dedicated to

S. Parkman Tuckerman, Esq.

BY

JOSEPH PHILIP KNIGHT.

Price 38 cts. nett.

BOSTON.

Published by OAKES & SWAN, 8½ Tremont Row.

Entered according to act of Congress in the year 1840 by Oakes & Swan in the Clerks office of the District Court of Massachusetts.

25   Robert Cooke (?–1843),
The Harrington Grand Quick Step, 1840.

Lithograph, printed by Benjamin W. Thayer, Boston, 11.8 x 15.8.
Music by Ireneus J. Solomons. Boston: Henry Prentiss, 1840.
Collection of the author.

One of the mainstays of American musical life in the 1840s was the singing family, a group of four to six vocalists who were personal relatives, or claimed to be. The best known and most successful of these were the Singing Hutchinsons, while others of note were the Bakers, the Rainers, and the Amphions. Their songs, often composed within the group, fused the moral precepts of hymns and spiritual songs with the sentiment and melodrama of popular ballads to support abolition, temperance, Christian missionary work, and other vital causes of the period. The title pages of their published songs were often decorated with a four-square picture of the group, stiffly lined up and appearing as formidable as they were reported to sound.

Robert Cooke's illustration is far more naturalistic than these and gives some sense of a performance in progress. It is an important document of the American theatre because it provides a rare interior view of the sort of small music hall common to all American cities and towns, often improvised and seldom long-lived. Far more modest in scale and entertainments than the major theatres such as New York's Bowery (pl. 30), the small hall served an important role in establishing theatre traditions in the United States by providing a stage for novice entertainers. The Harringtons left no important mark on history except, perhaps, through their appearance in this print. Cooke depicted the group and the members of the audience so specifically that there can be little doubt that he was there with sketch book in hand.

WHITLOCK'S COLLECTION of ETHIOPIAN MELODIES.

Entered according to Act of Congress in the Year 1846 by C. G. Christman in the Clerks Office of the District Court of the Southern District of N.Y.

AS SUNG WITH GREAT APPLAUSE BY

WILLIAM WHITLOCK

at the

PRINCIPAL THEATRES IN THE UNITED STATES

New York Published by C. G. Christman, 404 Pearl Street

31 Charles Parsons (1821–1910),
Slaying the Deer, 1847.

Lithograph, printed by George and William Endicott, New York, 26.6 x 19.6.
Music and words by Samuel Lover. New York: Firth, Hall & Pond, 1847.
American Antiquarian Society.

Charles Parsons came to New York from England as a child in 1830. In
1833, at the age of twelve, he was apprenticed to George Endicott. Two
years later, in respect to his skills and despite his tender age, he was
taken on as a regularly employed lithographic artist. He remained at
the Endicott shop until 1861, when he became head of the art department at the Harper publishing company. His music illustrations date
from the 1840s. They are always at least competent and sometimes, as
here, more than that. The double meaning of the title of Samuel Lover's
song is so strained a pun that it is just as well that there are two interesting vignettes to draw our attention away from it. In the hunt episode,
the dogs pursue the stag so hotly that he leaps out of the confines of
the illustration. The other picture is one of mood, a graceful sleighing
scene that stands as a quiet relief to its companion.

With this title page and that of *Knickerbocker Quadrilles* (pl. 28), we
have examples of one means of enlarging the role of pictorial matter on
the title page. Rather than one large illustration, which might over-
whelm the title proper, two or more smaller vignettes are used, enclosed
and connected by ornamental foliation. After the mid-1850s, worries
about title page proportions seem to have been set aside with the result
that symmetrical arrangements of multiple vignettes fade from
fashion.

M. Schmitz (act. 1840–1860),
"A Little More Grape Captain Bragg," 1847.

Lithograph, printed by P. S. Duval, Philadelphia, 15 x 19.8.
Music by William J. Lemon. Philadelphia: Lee & Walker, 1847.
American Antiquarian Society.

The many music illustrations of the 1840s and 1850s signed "M. Schmitz" are thought to be the work of Matthew Schmitz, a music teacher in Philadelphia about whom little is known. He was a first-rate copyist and some of his designs may be original, though the present example is not. It is a version of a standard American view of the Battle of Buena Vista in the Mexican War and had great currency in 1847, the year of the battle. Schmitz probably worked from prints issued by publishers in Philadelphia and elsewhere, though it is conceivable that he also had access to original drawings. His understanding and control of the possibilities of his medium was so great that this music illustration is superior as a print to some of the separately published and more expensive views of the same battle.

As was the practice of the time with battle art, the view is idealized. Because it occurred on unfamiliar ground and was won with relative ease, the Mexican War was widely and simply glorified. It provided some artists with an opportunity to show in idealized battle the colorful uniforms of the private militia companies, previously shown mostly in town and on parade grounds. This is not to say that the private companies actually went to war, however. The still life above the illustration is undoubtedly original with Schmitz. Its charm wanes somewhat when it becomes clear that except for the lateral leafy tendrils, it consists entirely of shot, cannon balls, a mortar, gunsmoke, and other signs of battle.

"A LITTLE MORE GRAPE CAPTAIN BRAGG"

P.S. Duval, Lith. Philad.ª

A NATIONAL SONG

Composed & respectfully dedicated to

GENERAL ZACHARY TAYLOR

by

Wᵐ. J. LEMON.

Price { Piano. 50 cts net
Guitar; 25 „ „

Philadelphia **LEE & WALKER** *120 Walnut Str.*
New Orleans **W. T. MAYO** *Nº 5. Camp Str.*

33 Unknown artist,
Knickerbocker Saloon Quick Step, 1849.

Lithograph, printed by William Sharp & Co., Boston, 15.5 x 22.5.
Music by Adam Stewart. Boston: Martin & Beals, 1849.
American Antiquarian Society.

The game of nine-pins had moved indoors from the bowling greens by
the 1840s and here, in 1849, we have a set of four alleys which have
the appearance of modern lanes. In this straightforward view with its
diligently worked out perspective, the artist has been careful to include
such touches of authenticity as a pin-boy and appropriately de-coated
bowlers. Though there is little of that sense of life which enlivens
Johnston's *Ice-Cream Quick Step,* there is a sure sense of place.

The artist may have been the printer, William C. Sharp, who should
not be confused with William Sharp (whose characteristic signature
may be seen in plate 22, *Freemens' Quick Step*), his third cousin and
rival as an artist, art teacher, and lithographic printer in Boston. The
brothers William C. and James C. Sharp were associated as lithographic
printers while their older cousin was associated variously with Francis
Michelin and Ephraim Bouvé.

Knickerbocker Saloon
QUICK STEP

W. SHARP & Co LITH.

PRICE 25 Cts NETT

COMPOSED AND RESPECTFULLY DEDICATED
TO THE
Proprietors
OF THE
KNICKERBOCKER SALOON.
BY
ADAM STEWART

Published by MARTIN & BEALS 184 Washington St

Entered according to Act of Congress in the year 1847 by Martin & Beals in the Clerks Office of the District Court of Mass.

CARICATURE SCHOTTISCHE,

E. Masson del.   Bufford's Lith. Boston.

Composed & dedicated to his friend

ALFRED JAELL,

BY

L'Aboyeur.

BOSTON.

Published by OLIVER DITSON, 115 Washington St.

Price 25 cts. net.   J.H. Bufford's Lith. Boston.

BERRY & GORDON	T. T. BARKER	D. A. TRUAX	C. C. CLAPP & CO.	J. E. GOULD
New York	Boston	Cinn.	Boston.	Philad.ª

40 George F. Bensell (1837–1879),
Christmas Schottisch, 1855.

Lithograph, printed with tint by Thomas Sinclair, Philadelphia, 28.5 x 20.9.
Music by George L. Walker. Philadelphia: Edward L. Walker, 1855.
American Antiquarian Society.

George Frederick Bensell, a native of Philadelphia, was eighteen when
he created this fascinating example of music title design. It is a fine
exercise in the then-current vogue for rustic ornamentation. The
half-surround of branches and twigs draws from popular adaptations
of the picturesque and the gothic, combining them in a free imitation of
baroque strapwork. In both Britain and America in the 1840s and
1850s, this was a popular mode of decoration, particularly favored by
illustrators of books and music because of its advantage of giving the
feel of a border without actually enclosing a vignette with a hard edge,
which would tend to diminish the sense of informality. Bensell's use of
bent limbs to form words is part of the style, though his penchant to
suspend some letters from branches while levitating others is not. His
title design for Walker's *Woodburn Polka* (1855) takes the rustic mode
into summer and thereby adds foliage and fruit to the decorative
possibilities.

Bensell's illustration is of a snowball fight, watched over by a snowman-
Father Christmas figure whose melting shape is echoed in the odd
anatomy of the uppermost boy. The year following this design, Bensell
began exhibiting at the Pennsylvania Academy and soon became
well-regarded as a painter of landscapes.

Designed by Geo F. Bensell.

Entered according to act of Congress A.D. 1855 by Edward L. Walker in the Clerks Office of the District Court for the Eastn Distt Pa.

Pr. 25 Cts nett.

T. Sinclair's lith Phila

41 Winslow Homer (1836–1910),
The Ratcatcher's Daughter, 1855.

Lithograph, printed with tint by John H. Bufford, Boston, 28.8 x 22.5.
Music and words arranged by Sam Cowell. Boston: Oliver Ditson, n.d.
Collection of the author.

Winslow Homer's first assignments as an apprentice at J. H. Bufford's
lithographic printing shop were to copy onto stone title page illustrations for songs that had been published earlier in the 1850s and were
about to be republished: *Katy Darling, O Whistle and I'll Come to You
My Lad,* and *Annie Lawrie* [sic]. He added nothing new except his
initials in *Katy* and *Annie.* Once settled into his job, he began to break
the shackles of straight copywork by extensively altering the designs
of those prints he was assigned to copy. Among the earliest of his litho-
graphs to be original in any important way is the present title page,
which was published in December 1855.

Homer's design is an adaptation of the title page of the Davidson
edition published in London in 1855 when the traditional song had
gained new popularity, largely through its performances by the entertainer, Sam Cowell. With minor changes, Homer retained two major
elements of the wood engraving after a drawing by W. A. Barrett that
served the Davidson edition. These are the undulating ribbon of rats
and the central figure of Cowell as the ratcatcher with his backdrop
setting of St. Paul's Cathedral and London Bridge. The three cats and
their prey, who do not figure in the song in any way, are original with
Homer as are two of the donkeys—Barrett had included only the head
of the central animal. In all respects Homer's draughtsmanship is surer
and the design is more interesting than his English model, but of course
he had the advantages of lithography and was not at the mercy of the
unknown wood engraver who subjected Barrett's design to near-
mutilation. With this example we find Homer having broken from the
confines of copywork sufficiently to leave the mark of his own person-
ality on the re-made illustration. The galloping donkey is pure Homer.

His initials are part of the tint, lower left, so that they are not found on
those states of the lithograph that are without a tint or that have a
different tint pattern.

THE RATCATCHER'S DAUGHTER

COMPOSED BY
SAM. COWELL.
BOSTON.
Published by OLIVER DITSON 115 Washington St.

J.H.Bufford's Lith Boston.

48   Unknown artist,
     The Ledger Polka, 1859.

Lithograph, printed by P. S. Duval & Son, Philadelphia, 15.6 x 15.6.
Music by James Bellak. Philadelphia: Beck & Lawton.
American Antiquarian Society.

It seems likely that this piece was issued for reasons of vanity as much
as for advertising, or as a friendly gesture from one publisher to another. Whatever the motive, the result was a fine illustration of life
on a Philadelphia street corner. The firmly outlined figures and the
mixing of very specific portraits such as the two men at the doorway
to the Ledger office with caricatures such as the dwarf and the boy,
suggest an experienced talent at work. John L. Magee, Emile Masson,
and M. Schmitz are possibilities, though there are not enough stylistic
similarities with the known work of any of them to warrant an attribution. Most of the faces would have been familiar to many Philadelphia
viewers in 1859, so that the title page would have had an impact similar
to a news photo in the twentieth century.

THE
LEDGER POLKA.

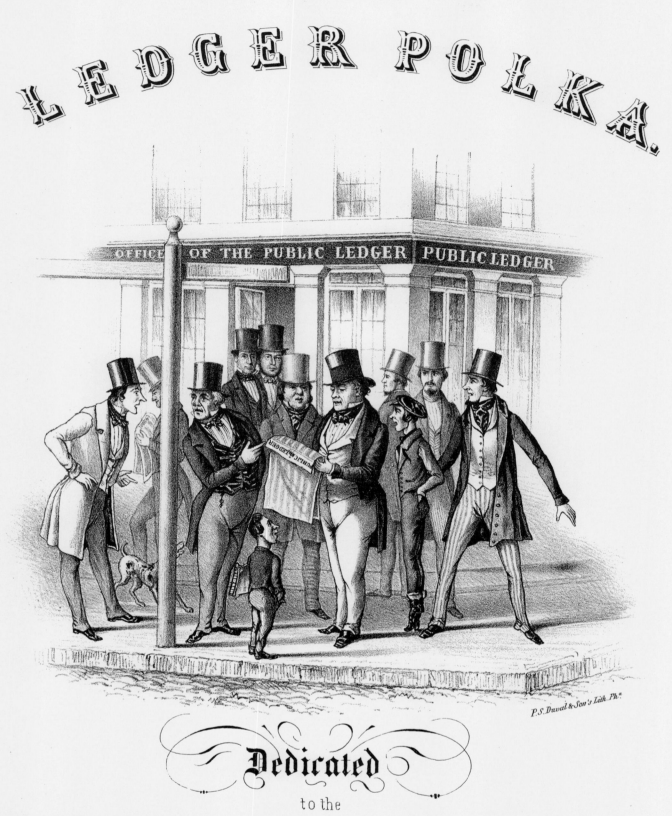

Dedicated

to the

READERS of the PUBLIC LEDGER Philad^a.

by

JAMES BELLAK.

Philad^a. Published by BECK & LAWTON, 166, Chesnut St. Cor. 7th
Successors to J.E. GOULD

Boston. OLIVER DITSON & CO.   New-York, S.T. GORDON.   TRUAX & BALDWIN, Cincinnati.

49   Unknown artist,
The Staten Island Gentleman, 1859.

Lithograph, printed in colors by Sarony, Major and Knapp, New York, 17 x 15.
Music arranged by Thomas Baker; words by Champion Bissell. New York:
    Firth, Pond & Co., 1859.
American Antiquarian Society.

It has always seemed fair to poke fun at the universal and eternal plight of the commuter. In this comic ballad, Bissell dwells on such benefits of commuting from Staten Island to New York City as rising early, contending with mud-filled roads while racing for the ferry, and shopping for one's suburb-bound wife. The illustration shows a commuter who has just completed the last of these activities, having spent much of the day away from his office following a preposterous shopping list. He now races for the last boat home, ". . . hung round with packages . . . a market basket on each arm. . . . A daily amateur express is a Staten Island Gentleman." With the quiet panic allowed a man of his station, our hero sprints for the ferry, fearful of missing it and fearful as well of his wife's response when she confirms what he suspects, that he has bought the wrong colors and sizes, forgot what she most wanted, and has lost the chops they were to have for dinner.

The shop windows, street post, and building façades provide a static vertical background for the flying figure of the commuter. The onlookers mirror the viewer's own amusement at the illustration. Some of the letters of the title are formed from images taken from the song, including the ferryboat which the poor soul is bound to miss.

THE
STATEN ISLAND
GENTLEMAN

COMIC BALLAD

WORDS BY

ENTERED ACCORDING TO ACT OF CONGRESS IN THE YEAR 1859 BY FIRTH, POND & Cº IN THE CLERKS OFFICE OF THE DISTRICT COURT OF THE SOUTHⁿ DISᵀ OF N.Y.

CHAMPION BISSELL.

INSCRIBED BY PERMISSION TO

Mrs C. C. Norvell, New Brighton, S.I.

LITH. OF SARONY, MAJOR & KNAPP, 449 BROADWAY, N.Y.

MUSIC ARRANGED FROM NOCTES AMBROSIANÆ BY

THOMAS BAKER.

NEW YORK.
PUBLISHED BY FIRTH, POND & Cº 547 BROADWAY.

ROCHESTER.
J. P. SHAW.

NEW HAVEN.
SKINNER & SPERRY.

BOSTON.
OLIVER DITSON & CO.

CINCINNATI.
C. Y. FONDA.

EN AVANT!

CINCINNATI,
Published by **A.C. PETERS & BRO.** Nº 94 **West Fourth Str.**, opposite the Post Office
Successors to W.C. PETERS & SONS
ST. LOUIS, MO., J.L. PETERS & BRO.

55   Unknown artist,
Bugaboo Schottisch, 1865.

Lithograph, printed with tint by A. Hoen & Co., Baltimore, 23 x 20.1.
Music by Albert Holland. Baltimore: Henry McCaffrey, 1865.
American Antiquarian Society.

Although a common initial reaction to this illustration is to think that
monstrous changes have befallen Santa Claus, the grotesque figure is,
of course, the bogey-man, hard at work collecting misbehaved children
whose worst fears have been realized and who now face unspeakable—
and unknown—fates. Since the quotient of humor in this grim fantasy
is heavily outweighed by its repellent qualities, we may be sure that
the piece was not bought for the charm of its title page. No, the women
who bought it doubtless intended to use it to terrify their tots into
diligence at piano practice.

Bugaboo Schottisch.

Lith. by A. Hoen & Co. Baltimore.

COMPOSED BY

ALBERT HOLLAND.

BALTIMORE,

PUBLISHED BY HENRY McCAFFREY, No 205, BALTIMORE ST.

56 Samuel S. Frizzell (1843–1895),
Croquet, 1866.

Lithograph, printed by F. N. Carter, Boston, 28.5 x 23.5.
Caption title: *The Nicest Kind of Croquet.*
Music by Christobel. Boston: G. D. Russell, 1866.
American Antiquarian Society.

In the 1860s and 1870s, S. S. Frizzell, along with Joseph E. Baker and
others, specialized in pictorial titles in which the vignette covered virtually the entire page and the title was an integral part of it, drawn
in the same style as the pictorial matter. The drawing of features,
foliage, and shadows was characterized by a softness enhanced by the
use of soft lithographic crayon on grained zinc plates, which had begun
to supplant limestone for much lithographic printing. The style chiefly
served a melodramatic sentimentalism, a quality which seems subdued
in Frizzell's *Croquet* in contrast with the standards of an age which
wore its sentimentalism on its sleeve.

Soon after the importation of the game of croquet from England
around 1860, it became a national pastime and one of the few outdoor
sports in which both men and women could participate. The game
quickly became part of the ornate formalities of courtship and a spate
of popular songs followed, linking the novelty of the game to the sentiment of young love. The lyricist of this song archly tells of looking to
see what the new game was all about and spying a couple seated,
"...his arm around her waist in a loving way ... Was *that* croquet?"

Doughty, Thomas (1793–1856)
    Centennial Dirge. Francis Johnson. Philadelphia: the author, 1832.

Fabronius, Dominique C. (?–aft. 1887)
    Gottschalk Waltz. T. Carreno. Boston: Ditson, 1863.

Frizzell, Samuel S. (1843–1895)
    Fairy Wedding. J. Turner. Boston: Ditson, n.d.
    Little Sunshine. C. White. Boston: White, Smith & Perry, 1873.
56 *Nicest Kind of Croquet*. Christabel. Boston: G. Russell, 1866.
    Stars of Heaven. G. Wheeler. Boston: White, Smith & Co., 1875.

Grozelier, Leopold (1830–1865)
    Dreaming, Ever Dreaming. Root. Boston: Russell & Tolman, n.d.
38 *Dying Words of Little Katy*. H. Waters. New York: H. Waters, 1853.
    Echo. A. Bendelari. Boston: Russell & Fuller, 1858.
    Gov. Banks' Grand March. J. Turner. Boston: Ditson, 1857.
    Saucy Kate. G. Benkert. Philadelphia: Piot, n.d.
    Still in My Dreams Thou'rt Near. F. Hall. Boston: Russell & Tolman, n.d.

Hoen, Ernest (act. 1846–aft. 1860)
    Ingleside Gallopade. A. Metz. Baltimore: Willig, 1847.
    La Creole. T. Wilson. Baltimore: Miller & Beacham, 1854.

Homer, Winslow (1836–1910)
    Annie Lawrie. Boston: Ditson, n.d.
    Katy Darling. Boston: Ditson, n.d.
42 *Lisette Polka Mazurka*. A. Talexy. Boston: Ditson, 1856.
    Minnie Clyde. L. Crosby. Boston: Ditson, 1857.
    O Whistle and I'll Come to You My Lad. J. Bruce. Boston: Ditson, n.d.
    Queen's Waltzes. C. D'Albert. Boston: Ditson, 1856.
41 *Ratcatcher's Daughter*. S. Cowell. Boston: Ditson, n.d.
    Rogers Quick Step. A. Dodworth. New York: H. Dodworth, 1856.
    Star Spangled Banner. No. [6] of *National Songs of America*. arr. F. Brown. Boston: Ditson, 1856.
43 *Wheelbarrow Polka*. Boston: Ditson, 1856.
    Wreath. H. Schwing. Boston: Ditson, n.d.

Hoppin, Augustus (1828–1896)
    Whisper of Love. F. Brown. New York: Hall, 1855.

Inman, Henry (1801–1846)
10 *Major Jack Downing's March*. J. Norton. Philadelphia: the author, c. 1833.

Johnston, David Claypoole (1798–1865)
    Coal Black Rose. Boston: D. C. Johnston, n.d.
 9 *Corner-stone March*. C. Zeuner. Boston: Bradlee, 1832.
27 *Ice-Cream Quick Step*. J. Garcia. Boston, 1841.
 5 *Log House*. A. P. Heinrich. Boston, 1826.
 4 *Massa Georgee Washington and General Lafayette*. M. Hawkins. New York: E. Riley, 1824.
    Rangers Quick Step. T. Comer. Boston: Bradlee, 1834.
    Schoolmaster. Boston: Parker & Ditson, 1839.
 7 *Storia d'un Violino. Trillo di Yankeedoodle*. A. P. Heinrich. London: 1831.

Koellner, August (1813–?)
    Ashland Quick Step. Ratel. Philadelphia: 1844.

Lane, Fitz Hugh (1804–1865)
    Ariel Waltz. T. Comer. Boston: Oakes & Swan, n.d.
17 *Captn. E. G. Austin's Quick Step*. arr. T. Comer. Boston: Parker & Ditson, 1837.
    Lawrence Quick Step. Kurek, arr. S. Knaebel. Boston: C. Keith, 1839.
19 *Mad Girl's Song*. H. Russell. Boston: Oakes & Swan, 1840.
    Maniac. H. Russell. Boston: Parker & Ditson, 1840.
    Mariner's Return. B. Baker. Boston: Reed, 1841.

Mariner Loves O'er the Waters to Roam. A. Lee. Boston: Ditson, n.d.

Norfolk Guards Quick Step. G. Farmer. Boston: Oakes & Swan, 1840.

14 *Nahant Quadrilles.* J. Hewitt. Philadelphia: Nunns, 1836.

Old Arm Chair. H. Russell. Boston: Oakes & Swan, 1840.

On Ellen's Bosom Blushed a Rose. T. Wiesenthal. Boston: Oakes & Swan, 1840.

Pesky Sarpent. Boston: Oakes & Swan, n.d.

Salem Mechanick Light Infantry Quick Step. J. Holloway. Salem: Ives & Putnam, 1836.

Song of the Fisher's Wife. G. Farmer. Boston: Oakes & Swan, 1840.

Lewis, Charles (act. 1838–1842)

21 *Tippecanoe, the Hero of North Bend.* New York: T. Birch, 1840.

Magee, John L. (1824–aft. 1868)

National Polka Quadrilles. W. Coleman. Philadelphia: Lee & Walker, 1857.

Masson, Emile (act. 1851–1862)

53 *Brilliant Polka.* L. Engleke. Philadelphia: J. Gould, 1862.

39 *Caricature Schottische.* L'Aboyeur. Boston: Ditson, 1854.

Miller, Alfred Jacob (1810–1879)

11 *Far O'er the Deep Blue Sea.* J. Hewitt. Baltimore: Willig, 1834.

The Warrier Crossed the Ocean's Foam. C. Meineke. Baltimore: Willig, 1836.

Nast, Thomas (1840–1902)

58 *Celebrated Arion Carnival Festival March.* C. Faust. N.Y.: J. Schuberth, 1867.

Newell, John P. (c. 1830–1898)

Grave of Kitty Clyde. C. Osborne. Boston: Russell & Tolman, 1859.

Newsam, Albert (1809–1864)

Monterey. No. 1 of *Parlor Duets.* J. Viereck. Philadelphia: Fiot, 1846.

Abd-El-Kader Quick Step. J. Viereck. Philadelphia: Fiot, 1844.

Dreams of Home. A. B. Durand. Philadelphia: Lee & Walker, 1852.

He's on the Sea. G. Rodwell. Philadelphia: Lee & Walker, n.d.

Never Despair. J. Braham. Philadelphia: Fiot, 1852.

Palmer, Frances Bond (c. 1812–1876)

Peace of Home. J. Benedict. New York: Millet, n.d.

Spanish Gipsies Polka. H. Griffiths. New York: Gould & Berry, n.d.

Parsons, Charles (1821–1910)

Beautiful Flowers of May. A. Lee. New York: Firth & Hall, 1846.

Bohemian Girl Quadrilles. M. Balfe, arr. A. Dodworth. New York: Firth, Hall & Pond, 1844.

Devilshoof Quick Step. Balfe, arr. A. Dodworth. New York: Firth, Hall & Pond, 1845.

Mahopac Lake Waltz. A. Dodworth. New York: Firth, Hall & Pond, 1845.

Mountain Home Quick Step. F. Brown, arr. S. Dyer. New York: Hall, 1847.

Ocean Wave Quick Step. A. Dodworth. New York: Firth & Hall, 1843.

Oh Charming May. G. Rodwell. New York: Hall, 1846.

31 *Slaying the Deer.* S. Lover. New York: Firth, Hall & Pond, 1847.

Sweet Afton Water. W. Wetmore. New York: Millet, n.d.

Penniman, John (c. 1817–1850)

Odd Fellows' Greeting. Orphean. New York: Atwill, 1845.

Rose Without a Thorn. W. Kirby. Baltimore: Cole, n.d.

Queen, James (1821–1886)

Beautiful May. A. Lee. Philadelphia: Ferrett, n.d.

Dreams of the Past. Six Songs. J. Duggan. Philadelphia: Klemm, 1844.

Jeannie Gray. C. Mueller. Philadelphia: Walker, 1849.

My Annie O. W. Bateman. Philadelphia: Walker, 1850.

35 *New Costume Polka.* M. Keller. Philadelphia: Lee & Walker, 1851.

Phoenix Quick Step. V. Vallue. Philadelphia: Walker, 1849.

Saratoga Galop. G. Blessner. Philadelphia: Willig, 1841.

Star Spangled Banner. arr. C. Voss. Philadelphia: Andre, 1861.

Washington Light Infantry Quick Step. M. Zuboff. Philadelphia: Meignen.

Rimmer, William (1816–1879)
16 *Fireman's Call*. Boston: Keith, 1837.
15 *Roarers*. J. Holloway. Boston: Keith, 1837.

Rowse, Samuel Worcester (1822–1901)
Blue E'ed Lassie. J. Willis. Boston: Oakes, 1841.
He Led Her to the Altar. B. Barclay. Philadelphia: Fiot, 1842.
Lestocq. Auber. Boston: Oakes, n.d.
Malibran Waltz. Parker. Boston: Prentiss, 1841.
National Whig Song. W. Hayden. Boston: Parker & Ditson, 1840.
Southerner Quick Step. H. Oates. Charleston: G. Oates, 1847.

Sanford, George (act. 1837–1847)
Dodworth's Knickerbocker Quadrilles. A. Dodworth. New York: Firth & Hall, 1846.
18 *Striped Pig*. New York: Hewitt & Jacques, 1838.
Time! Thou Cheat of Human Bliss. Rooke. New York: Firth & Hall, n.d.
Yes, Methinks I See Her Smiling. Rooke. New York: Firth & Hall, n.d.

Sarony, Napoleon (1821–1896)
The Swiss Girl. G. Linley. New York: Kerksieg & Breusing, 1848.

Schmitz, M[atthew?] (act. 1840–1860)
32 *"A Little More Grape Captain Bragg."* W. Lemon. Philadelphia: Lee & Walker, 1847.
California, or Gold! T. Pearce, Philadelphia: Lee & Walker, n.d.
Fairies' Revelry. Ehrlich. Philadelphia: Walker, 1848.
Identical Polka. J. Darling. Philadelphia: Lee & Walker, 1853.
Rough and Ready. A. Schmitz. Philadelphia: Lee & Walker, n.d.
'Tis Night, My Bark is on the Ocean. S.D.S. Philadelphia: Perring, 1845.
Tom Pouce Quadrilles. J. Duvernoy. Philadelphia: Willig, n.d.
Virginia Melodies for the Flute. A. Kyle. New York: Nunns, 1844.

Sharp, William (c. 1802–aft. 1862)
Fairest Maid on Devon's Banks. J. White. Boston: Prentiss, 1841.
Fleurs d'Été. F. David. Boston: Wade, 1849.
22 *Freemens' Quick Step*. G. Hews. Boston: Parker & Ditson, 1840.
Withered Tree. G. Rodwell. Boston: Oakes, n.d.

Smith, A. C. (act. 1831–1856)
Log Cabin Quick Step. Baltimore: Willig, 1840.
Odd Fellows March. J. Hewitt. Baltimore: Willig, 1838.

"Spoodlyks" (act. 1836–1846)
Gingerbread Man. arr. J. Dobney. New York: Endicott, 1836.
28 *Knickerbocker Quadrilles*. arr. H. Dodworth. New York: Firth & Hall, 1843.
Santa Claus' Quadrilles. arr. H. Dodworth. New York: Firth, Pond, 1846.
Whar Did You Come From. J. Sweeney. New York: Firth & Hall, 1840.

Stone, Henry (act. 1822–1846)
Coleridge's Song on Peace. Washington?, c. 1823.
2 *Maid of the Rock*. Washington?, c. 1823.
Miscellaneous Lesson. Washington?, c. 1823.
They're A'Noddin. Wagler. Washington?, c. 1823.
(The above four titles are included in a collection of vocal and instrumental music thought to be published by Stone in Washington c. 1823. Wolfe 2002.)
The Generous Chief. [J. Mazzinghi.] arr. I. Hutton. Washington, 1823.

Swett, Moses (act. 1826–1837)
Boys of Kilkenny. New York: J. Hewitt, 1835.
Hark! Hark! The Soft Bugle. M. S. Baltimore: Willig, 1831.
Knight from Palestine. J. Hewitt. Baltimore: Willig, n.d.
Oh Mount Thy Bright and Gallant Steed. J. Hewitt. Baltimore: Willig, 1831.
Texian Grand March. E. Meyrick. New York: Firth & Hall, 1836.

Walcutt, William (1819–1882)
Lilac at the Door. W. Wetmore. New York: W. Hall, 1857.

Weir, Robert W. (1803–1889)
Splendor Falls on Castle Walls—The Echo Song. J. Barnard, arr. A. Apelles. New York: Pond, 1864.
Sweet and Low—The Cradle Song. J. Barnard, arr. A. Apelles. New York: Van Nostrand, 1864.

Welcker, F. (act. 1854–1876)
Gossip and Report. F. Wilson. St. Louis: Balmer & Weber, n.d.
Scotia. F. Woolcott. St. Louis: Harlow, 1862.
Very Crooked Whiskey March. St. Louis: Balmer & Weber, 1876.

Whateley, Horace (act. 1859–1862)
Douglas's Funeral March. J. Hewitt. Philadelphia: Lee & Walker, 1861.
Lincoln Quick Step. C. Grobe. Philadelphia: Lee & Walker, 1860.
Louisa Miller Quadrille. Roquette. Philadelphia: Lee & Walker, n.d.
Major Anderson's Grand March. Philadelphia: Lee & Walker, 1861.
Tolling Bell. C. Grobe. Philadelphia: Lee & Walker, 1859.
Zouave Grand Parade March. Philadelphia: Lee & Walker, 1861.

Whistler, James Abbott McNeill (1834–1903)
36 *Song of the Graduates.* A. Apelles. New York: Firth, Pond, 1852.